Still Beautiful

Still Beautiful

THE COLOR OF BEAUTY

KEVIN BATES

LitPrime Solutions
21250 Hawthorne Blvd
Suite 500, Torrance, CA 90503
www.litprime.com
Phone: 1-800-981-9893

Published by LitPrime Solutions   01/17/2023

ISBN: 979-8-88703-111-8(sc)
ISBN: 979-8-88703-112-5(e)

Library of Congress Control Number: 2022923183

Contents

SECTION 2
Through the Fire (Tribute to My Son Michael Grenzer)

SECTION 3
Sad & Painful

SECTION 4
Mary's Goodbye

Thanks & Dedication

My thanks go to the Almighty God, who has given me the gift of words, life, and happiness to share his greatness with others. Thank you God for the great "Gifts of Life", my family and friends, who make me stronger in my faith. Thank you, Jesus Christ who died for our sins so we would be better people. Thank you Apostle David Roberson and Prophetess Wanda Roberson of the Empowerment Center for being great leaders and teachers in the word of God while helping me to walk in faith daily and stay on the path my mother and grandmother put me on.

I give a shout out to the music of the 60's and 70's that kept so many people together, singing and dancing while at the same time imparting a strong message. Thank you, Sly and the Family Stone, Sam Cook, O'Jays, Al Green, Bill Withers, Isley Brother, Temptations, Isaac Hayes, Last Poets, Marvin Gaye, Stevie Wonder and so many more. Love you all!

Lastly, I want to give a huge thanks to my family. The queen, my beautiful mother, Mary Bates. Her love sustains us. The oldest of the siblings, "The Sheriff," Karen Barnes. She kept order when my mother was away, cooked for us, made sure we did our school work and household chores. My younger brother, the rock & the wheel, Terrell Bates Sr. The rock, because as a kid he was so hard-headed and always got into trouble, as an adult he is a solid parent and God-fearing Christian man who can't be broken. The wheel, because no matter what obstacles come his way he keeps on rolling. My baby sister, the princess, Kimba Jackson, because as a baby she was so beautiful. We all knew from the moment she was born that one day she would inherit the scepter from the queen. My son, the survivor and overcomer, Michael Grenzer, who has seen the faults of those before him and has learned from them. Lastly, a huge thanks to 'my brother from another mother', "The Hand", Stephen Cole, the artist.

Thank You Family!

A special dedication goes out to professors and poets, Nikki Giovanni and Maya Angelou. Every time I hear them speak, they make me smile, think, and write.

The heart of my dedication goes to family we have lost and those who are still here; because it is strong family love that made me aware of self and those around.

I dedicate this book to family past: Leo and Selena Green, Clarence "Butch" Turner Jr, Brenda Green, Albert, Alma, Craig, and Michael Johnson, Ora Lee Avery, Lisbon and Walter Beatrice Newton, Edward Livingston Sr., Freddie. Lois Livingston, Edward Livingston Jr., Wade Bates Jr.

I dedicate this book to family members living: Mary Bates, Byron and Karen Barnes, Colin and Kimba Jackson, Linda Johnson, Sharon Johnson, Kenneth Turner, Eric Avery, Terrell Bates Sr. Mary Newton-Jones. I dedicate to family because they first said the words "Black is Beautiful & I'm Black and I'm Proud". Taught me to look in the mirror and say "yes!" Family gave each other the knowledge of the speakers fighting for a cause; instilled a thought into each other...

The reasons that we are here are to honor God by loving one another, helping every chance we get; doing it because it is the right thing to do, not to get something in return. God created a beautiful being like you to be honored and loved. I look at someone like you and see the REASONS to better myself, to honor God through. To say "I love God" by saying, "I love you!"

Section 1

GROWING UP FAMILY LOVE

Afro

I remember the day of the march
a small kid in a house full of adults.
They are moving fast, bumping around.

Everyone in their colorful dashiki shirts
men and women both with big afros.
Me, full of excitement wishing I could go.

They push me aside saying, "stay outta way"
yet, my mother looking the best, with the biggest afro.
There with mine plaited, waiting to comb out.

Bringing mother a glass of water I walk in
on a lady putting on a nice big afro wig.
I'm shocked, I ask mother why must she do it?

Mother pulls me aside with her loving grace,
she say, "when we march the evil man pulls
out his clubs, stick, hoses and big dogs".

"We get beat for marching for our equal rights,
the afro cushions the hard blows and falls.
It's dangerous and that's why you can't go".

Black Ball

Most were expected to know their place
Don't ever dare challenge the master race
There are those you are smarter and better
Black men just were inferior to white men

This seems to be the thinking some time ago
Sports and recreation were for the privileged
Those who were stronger, mind and body
So athletics were played by the empowered

Before there was Sweetness, Air, Magic or Iron
A lesser known pioneer by the name of "The Major"
One of eight children, he found a way to stand out
He took to two wheels and rode to great success

Black man became the fastest cyclist of his time
Celebrated abroad, applauded by athletes
In U.S.A. things were thrown at him during a race
Southern states he couldn't race against Caucasians

Arthur Ashe won the U.S. and Australian Open
Then won Wimbledon against great Jimmy Connors
Achievements superseded his ability to swing a racket
Heart surgeries never depleted Arthur's grand heart

He founded the ATP with several players in 1969
This foundation awards players high prize money today
Fought to end apartheid and bring awareness to AIDS
A great man in the tennis world and the world around him

Jackie Robinson stole bases, just as he stole our hearts
My heart also goes out to Henry (Hammer) Aaron
Who was as strong as nails after the death threats he endured
Chasing the home run record of George Herman (Babe Ruth)

Before Ali proclaimed himself as the "Greatest" to step in the ring
Jack Johnson had made a place for black men between the ropes
It's said former slaves were put in their place when they lost
Johnson won a title in 1908, people called for a "Great White Hope"

Jack Johnson was called "subhuman ape", and should be beaten
That changed in 1910 when Jack became heavyweight champ
Jack Johnson and Joe Louis paved the way for many fighters
From their victories, we enjoy Ali, Frazer, Foreman & Jones Jr

Blacks could not quarterback, thought to be not smart enough
Doug Williams and Warren Moon changed that way of thinking
They were allowed to play, but no way could they coach
Black coaches and General Managers won the Super Bowl

What's been proven is it takes heart and determination
They must endure what the normal person cannot do
I honor their great strength and unbelievable courage
Fred Slater, Willie O'Ree, Earl Lloyd, and Jackie Robinson.

Author's Comments:

A lot of sports players today think they have it so hard. They go out to clubs and start fights. Repeatedly get into trouble, and go into the stands and start fights. Players before them were called nigger, coon, and spat upon. Death threats because they played a sport. Honor them and show the haters in the stands that you are better than them.

Black History

No welcome signs for my people when they arrived
Never asked if they wanted to come, so they were taken
Not given any land, so they cultivated it for another

Feed my children books full of stories they wrote
Paid some sort of tribute by giving us a month
Like it's only important to learn of my people once a year

I will know the truth because I will seek knowledge
They beat our men and work them 18 hours a day
Rape our women as if they were to be used and abused

Called you Bitches, Whores and Niggers with hate
We found some way to say and rap about it with love
I prefer to not speak it, Call you "Kings & Queens"

I know the Chinese built the railroads of this land
Yet, I'll talk about the one of my lady Harriet Tubman
Mission after mission risking her life to free others
Maybe it was the beatings she took or the weight to her head
She would return to risk her life to free so many others
A bounty put on her head to give others what they deserve

My sweet lady Harriet Jacobs also with a bounty
Tired of years of sexual harassment by a doctor no less
Found her way to the freedom that she righteously deserved

Said to have escaped without known reason or provocation
As if slavery or rape is not justification enough
To take one's body and dignity is not his God-given right

Grand women of the past who paved the way for many more
Numerous people more than I can begin to mention
A note of the past that made a way for those of now

Deborah Gray White understood what it was all about
Family is what brought the enslaved people together
"It made a woman a mother and a man a father".

'Family' words ingrained in my grandmother, the backbone.
My mother fought the wars of deceit to hold her 'Family' together
From Harriet Tubman to Selena Green and Mary Bates, I love you

Ladies first, in you all, I honor you all
I bow to you; admire your strength
Praise is due to the Queens of our past and now.

Authors Comments:

I did not mean to sound bitter but this is so hard to do. The subject
matter means so much to me; the battles that people before me fought
just as recent as one generation. I am much an aloof person but believe
in family. It teaches us respect and care. I love my family very much, but
do not tell my sisters that. Black people came together a family nation
and made a change. Let's remember them all, Female & Male.

Balance

I once lost my balance and fell,
oh boy, did that hurt so why try it?
Often times walking arms extended
people stop and wander, what's up.

Black men and white men have fought
then tried to separate, we need balance.
Total blackness we have darkness then
in complete whiteness we have blindness.

Just as the rough male needs the sweet female
for that connection to continue mankind.
That positive and negative to give off
the energy to go, go, go, like the bunny.

I may not love my enemy as the bible asks
yet I will practice the ways of my Lord.
My vilifier may not hate me and mine
although they practice in ways of evil
All about balance.

Blood Fruit

The slave master had a great orchard baring fruit;
it brought him riches under others' sweat and blood.
People working twelve hours a day chained and locked,
times he beat them with a whip to work harder for him.

Master of nothing he showed no skills at nothing but a whip.
The fruit his trees produced would sell to many foreign lands.
When the slave would attempt to run or grew old and weak
he would hang them from his tree just to make an example.

Blood ran into the ground from the beatings and hangings.
The trees grew fuller producing more leaves and fruit.
Soil becoming as rich as the souls tending on it daily,
when you cut into the fruit it now has a blood red color.

Bus Ride

I'm standing in this heat Wait
ing at a predestinated spot
Continue to look down the street

So hot today must be over 105°
Even the birds are not flying today
My cold drink does not prevent the sweat

Here it comes I see it now
Must it stop at every stop before me?
Can't wait to feel that cool air

As it arrives we form a line
Must I be the last one?
I surely hope I get a seat

I enter greeted with a "Hello"
Start to scan for a seat
Defiantly more than I expected

Make a way to a seat up front
I sit with a question repeated in my head
Why all the black people sit in the back?

At the tender age of sixteen I was asked
Why do I sit up front?
When all the cool people are in back

What makes you so damn cool?
To ignore the struggle of those before you
Remember the grandmother of the revolution

ROSA PARKS
I've read the books and seen the movies
So many people band together to march
Had to carpool or walk miles to get to work

They had to break a system
Cripple a city's money input
Just to be treated equal

Rosa Parks, Martin Luther King, Jr and Malcolm
More than names you hear in February
People who started a change for your betterment

When I think I have it so hard
I look to my grandmother and mother
Realize I don't know what tough is

I know you have a choice
You so chose to sit in the back
I chose to honor those before me

In Rose Parks I honor and I praise
Thank God for her tired feet.

Bill of Sale

As I sit here on this humid night
I reflect on my short history here.
The biography of those before me,
who have bled tells a greater tale.

Those stripped of their freedom and rights
land of birth they did disappear.
In a boat secured under lock and key.
For money, cotton, and a bill of sale.

Coincidence

It's more than a coincidence...
That we've been called Niggers so long
We've embraced the word with love and grace
Words we speak and rap in songs

It's more than a coincidence...
Our women been called Bitches and Hos
It means nothing for us to speak it
God's greatest creation belittled and not honored

People before us fought long and hard
Stood tall, marched many miles with pride
To overcome these words of hate
To be known as people and not objects

Much blood was spilled in the streets
Knew we would overcome
Would be allowed through the same door
Looked up to and not down upon
It's more than a coincidence...
Been told we would amount to nothing
We strive for nothing through education
Selling our souls and drugs on the street

It's more than a coincidence...
Called Niggers, Bitches, and Hos
Instead of songs to overcome and uplift
It's songs of Drugs, Niggers, Bitches, and Hos

We must rise above these mindless thoughts
Realize the people who we are...
Doctors, Lawyers, Kings, Queens, Teachers, and Students
We are the leaders of the next generation.

Desirable

If a desirable object is bought and sold
was a great yearning for my ancestors.
Yet they were sold into slavery in chains
desire to have them work for the whites.

Value increase they were never neglected
much attention through whips and rapes.
Treated with much evil for many years
white man thought ok because he bought.

The slaves held many desires of their own
was to stop being beaten and break the chains.
Reward came slowly for some of the slaves
the railroad or some bought out of slavery.

Yet it took the paperwork of a white leader
to void the bill of sale of evil slave owners.

Black Wealth

There was a race held back through segregation
being told they were nothing, didn't belong.
Was in lower class housing and education.
Being called nigger and coon far too long.

Black wealth came in voices of the times
telling us to unite and oppose the hated.
So we marched and took on the courts
Withstood the firehoses and evil judges.

Black wealth was looking in the mirror
accepting the God given color of your skin.
Saying "Black is beautiful I am beautiful"
Standing, raised fist, "I'm Black and I'm Proud!"

Black wealth is black families coming together
on Sunday's and holidays sharing love.

Equal

They said separate but equal
only to justify their evil racism.
One look at the schools told you
they were not of equal conditions.

Textbooks were the throw-aways
from white schools when they finished;
find words like 'nigger & coon' in them.
Meant to mock and keep you in place.

So came a time for all evil to change
to take this fight to the highest courts.
Understanding it meant togetherness;
many haters oppose the new law now.

Not accepting rich and poor share a bond
all men are created equal under God.
Brown vs Board changed education for all;
togetherness, equality under God and country.
Proverbs 22:2

Children's Playground

Words fall on deaf ears,
Kevin cares not what number 7 goes into.
Tick Tock.

Know not what is being said,
Frank cares not who conquered what.
Tick Tock.

Everyone watching the clock,
the ring of that bell a welcome relief.
Tick Tock.

Ring, Ring, Ring!
Everyone crash the doors,
time for fun on the Children's Playground.

Stanley and Byron run the obstacle course,
up and over, just like today's soldiers.
Is today the day Stanley wins?

Liz and Betty off playing jacks,
talking about which boys are cute.
Wondering if he really knows?

Some are jumping rope
Others play kickball
Screams of joy everywhere

Ring, Ring, Ring!
Time to come back in,
a small crowd starts to gather.

Frank and Kevin engage in hand to hand.
What could have started this?
Cheers for one and the other.

It is all fun and games,
Until someone is called "A Dumb Nigger!"
All this on a Children's Playground.

Excuse Me

Excuse me governor…
If I may have your attention please,
it's been 80-plus years, yet time's due.
There comes a time for justice to be served.

There was a time when a lie and hatred
was deemed to be what many called justice.
No way to change History's evil past,
the future can have glory and it starts now.

Excuse me governor…
I hope it's not a bad time for you now,
just a favor for nine souls gone on to glory.
I beg your pardon to give nine pardons.

Author Comments:

This poem acknowledges that it took 80 years to pardon 9 black men who were wrongly accused and convicted of rapes of a pair of white women. Even when it's believed that these black men were innocent, there was no overturning the conviction because black lives did not matter. They finished their lives in prison to die.

Four Little Angels

It is a Sunday Morning,
No different than any other,
So it would seem.

Something special about today,
It's a little overcast,
Sign of the rains to come.

Daddy and Mom's little angels,
Wearing their Sunday's best,
Looking their best for the Lord.

Four little girls leave for church,
Each going their own way,
Lives about to be entwined forever.

As they enter the holy sanctuary,
Safe from the evils of the times,
So one would believe.

Parents planning out the day,
That is all about to change,
This day will live forever.

Thunder rolls in the distance,
Powerful enough to shake the ground.

No! Something bad has happen.
People start going outside their homes,
There's smoke in the distance,
Starting to fill the air.

Word is starting to pass on the street,
They have bombed 16th Street Church.
Oh my God! The Children!

Running down the street,
Hoping and praying for the best.
Please God! Let them be O.K.

Looking around,
Making a head count,
Some people are missing.

Rain of tears start to flow,
While you dig through ash.
Hoping to find your loved one ALIVE.

You enter the morgue,
To identify your child,
Such horror in front of your eyes.

Bodies that are burnt,
Broken in pieces,
Cement embedded in a kid's head.

Who would do such a thing?
Who would hate so much?
Questions you cannot answer.

"Life is hard as steel"
Lord's grace soft as cotton
When you're in Jesus arms.

You can burn a church,
Cannot burn a spirit.
Might extinguish a life,
Never a movement.

September 15, 1963
The day Four Little Girls,
Became Four Little Angels.

Confidence

When evil comes, it obstructs the path
making uncertain the road ahead of us.
Evil wants you unknowing and confuse
then it will feed you lies to follow him.

Our confidence must remain on God,
on all he has given and promised us eternally.
It is his written word that is the great truth
take it in your heart, believe, and walk by faith.

Don't let the chaos in life take you off your path.
Faith in what you don't see will bring you through.
God said he will walk among us and be our God.
We must have confidence in true faith, in the unseen.

Leviticus 26:12 & Hebrews 11:1

Famine

There was a famine over the land;
not one for a need of food or water.
It was a famine of the Lord's word
in a mass land of hatred and death.

A race of people wandered about
Trying to find the direction to go.
Yet not only is it just the oppressed
the cynics needed leadership also.

Dr. King was a spiritual compass;
feeding a nation hungry for the word.
When we stood lost and asked
"Where, Where do we go from here?"

Dr. King said, "don't worry, follow me."
"We go and march down their streets,
sit at their counters because they're ours too.
Thank you Dr. King for marching and pushing.

Amos 8:11-12

Fundamentals

Came together under strong attraction
spending much time with one another.
Working on their fundamentals of love;
core of the affair he was white, she black.

Told her she was more than just a trophy;
she's not a notch he's carving in his bedpost.
They share much warmth and compassion,
the fundamentals seem to be there for them.

As time passed emotions grew for the young lady
the fundamental element of acceptance failed.
Young man knew his family would not allow her.
Only approval was among a small group of friends.

It's a shame the relationship progressed no further
because of the one fundamental thing the lady
could not change the beautiful hue of her skin.
It was goodbye, yet to learn fundamental empathy.

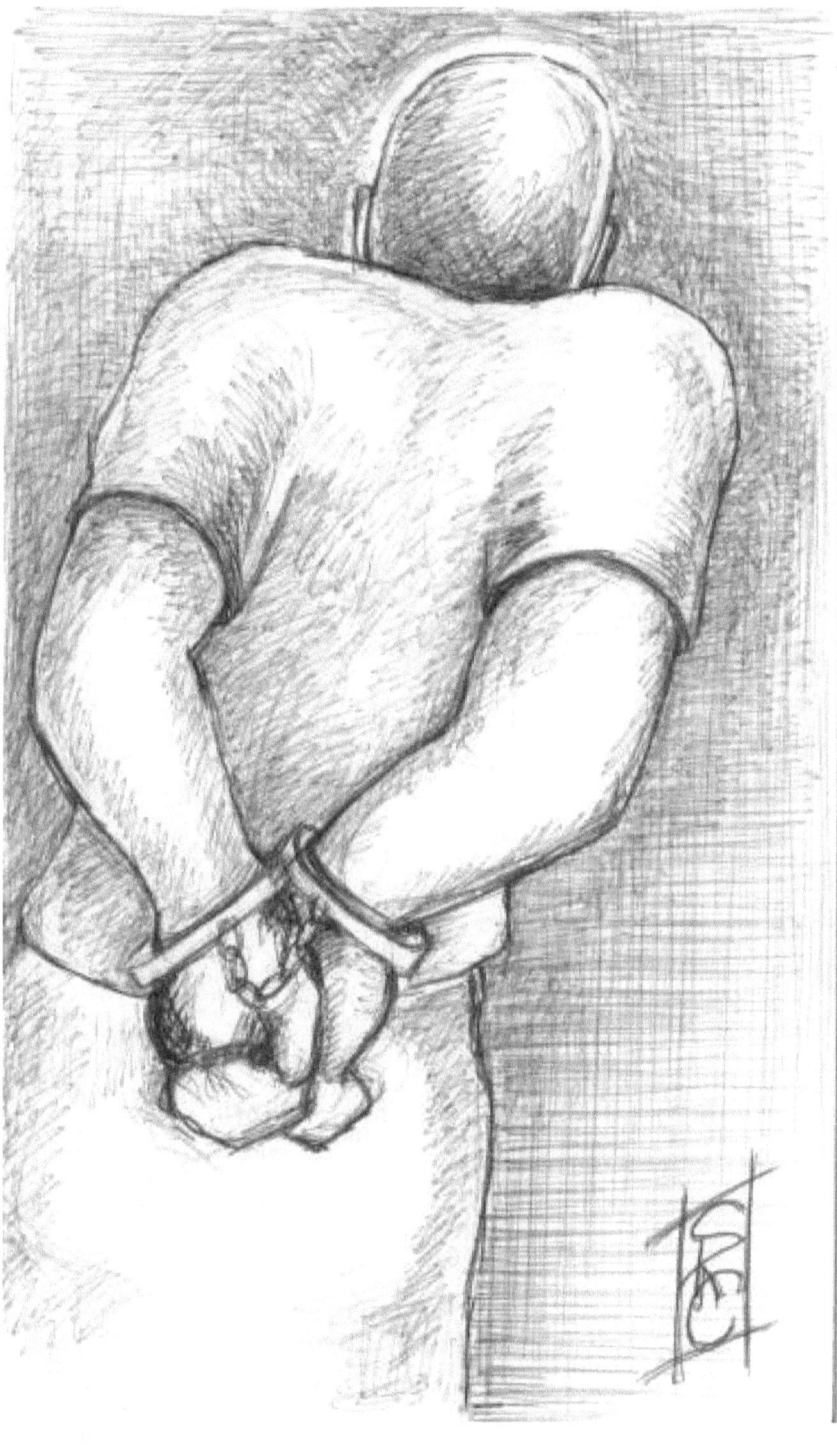

Cops and Robbers

Because as children it was a game
Later in life it was to become reality
Unleashing brute force, a bloody shame
Sticks and toy guns now clubs and 9mm
Hegemony to evil; life is never the same

When a cop takes a person's last breath
It's wrong when it's done out of hate
No more cops and robbers at playtime
Enjoyment of child's play is now death.

Hidden

Much admiration for my grandfather
Also, the great men of his generation.
Hidden pain and anger from family
being a great pillar of strength for us.

Living in a land of hate and deceit around
where judgement is passed by color of our skin.
Evil names are spoken often of our people
they see so much and hide their emotions.

We ask them, "How's your heart, do you not care;
do you see the things they do, and have
ears that hear all the evil things that are said?"
their reply is belief in a better world for you.

My grandfather knew food and a smiling face
made for a happy family and we push onward.
When he would talk about pain and anger of
the world, was on a bench with other old men.

Mark 8:18

High-Water Pants

Seven year-old running around having fun
playing ball with his friends afterschool.
In his collared shirt and high-water jean pants.

The jeans are a few inches short, yet it does
not bother the boy; they are new to him.
They are pressed and clean; he's looking sharp.

Single mom got them from a second-hand shop;
doing the best for the kids who she loves dearly.
They might wear high-waters, yet its hurricane season.

Hungry

She came through the door with authority
people noticed thought she was the po po.
Walked with her head held high, self-pride
yes she was full of herself she's done a lot.

When she was hungry for her education,
that need was met in the college system.
Young, beautiful, and with kids she'd push
forward late nights until she got her degree.

The kids were hungry screaming, "Momma
feed me we want to eat and feed the dog."
She'll say, "Shut up!" and make sure there
was enough food on the table for all to eat.

There came times when they were hungry
for the new fancy fashion trends out there.
Clothes were on their back to show everyone;
these kids were full of momma's LOVE!

 Injustice

Butler went to seek higher education
Lastly, he saw and felt was unjust racism
United they stood to change the legislation
Shut out the administration seemed to not care
Hunger and thirst for righteous was our salvation.

We're blessed because of the burning he went through
Ignite the passion for righteous and pray upon it
Never let evil be the victor in your life; God triumphs
Everyone stands, Jonathon, and says, "Thank you!"
Matthew 5:6

Author Comment:

This poem is left aligned because it is in a format called BLUSH WINE, which was created by me. In the first stanza, each line has 8-11 syllables, and the first, third, and last lines rhyme. In the last stanza, the first and last lines rhyme. Also, first letters of the two different stanzas spell BLUSH WINE.

This poem acknowledges Jonathon Butler, who seeks change in Ferguson, Missouri. The attention of what was going on in Ferguson made an impact of the injustice going on in other places. I used Matthew 5:6 "blessed are those who hunger & thirst for righteousness."

Knowing

Those around them always suspected,
never knowing the truth of this club.
They never would judge just wander.
Eyes and ears spoke, yet action was truth.

Standards were set long ago, then upheld,
came from the four corners of university.
To be told, "no, you are not wanted here",
sent away as unequal is personal to them.

So the club made racist songs and chants,
shouted and laughed, had much fun with it.
Saying, "never, never, never, you don't belong",
hatred widespread coming from lands afar.

When it comes back and affects the shouters,
then there is a claim of sorrow for the chants.
Is the sorrow genuine or a cover up of truth?
we sit, knowing hatred is the base of this club.

Author Comment:

This poem is left aligned because it is in a format called BLUSH WINE,
which was created by me. In the first stanza, each line has 8-11 syllables,
and the first, third, and last lines rhyme. In the last stanza, the first
and last lines rhyme.

Conductor

God is a fine conductor of life.
We're the orchestra waiting for
His direction for us to follow.
Sitting with hope, looking up baffled.

Just as the music is on a sheet;
The word of God is in the bible.
Written for us to follow in faith
Deliver us from evil to the empire.

The words are God waving his
Arms like the greatest conductor.
Creating great music in unison
Inspiring all who listen intently.

Lady Licorice

You have come to be known as L. L.
yeah that's my sister Lady Licorice.
She's rare in the pack, black, and strong.

As a baby they came from miles to see you
great outreach to have you in their hands.
Small and compact with a shiny black head.

Making your strong demands as a kid
we were quick to reply to Baby Licorice.
Always asking questions to gain knowledge.

Transform into a mother and teacher of hope,
smart lady, sure of self, and strong heritage.
Teaching to others as they come in her circle.

Lady Licorice is small, black, and strong
Feels good in your hands if you are lucky.
Yet, her power can only be handled by few.

Liberty

Saw herself as a neglected weed;
any good gardener she removed
herself from her master's flowers.

Never knowing of liberty she was
ignorant of its greatness to come.
She would share it with many more.

Harriet Tubman knew the sin against her
race; they were being taken from their home
then put into slavery in another land.

She led many to their new found liberty
on a smooth running railroad to promise.
As Moses said, "Set my people free!"

Just as descendants of Abraham believed.
Harriet believed her brethren and sisters
have never been slaves to anyone.

Clipper Sails

When words of the greats were spoken
Fifteen men of different skin banded
Stepped onto the court as their ship
Once again to fight for fans of love

Sailed from land to land many times
On a court to fight foes of a fun game
Then one day hated of the devil spoke
With love in their heart they united

The danger in their voyage came in
Choice of how to protest this evil
So Paul and his friends fought for
Who supports God's beautiful creation
The Clipper sailed on.

Authors Comments:

This poem is about how the L.A. Clipper players came together to protest against their owner Donald Sterling for the racist comments he made to his girlfriend. Donald stated he was living in a culture that causes him to feel a certain way towards blacks. He demanded his girlfriend to not bring blacks to his team's games. Clipper player, Chris Paul led his teammates to half-court during pre-game, to lay their jerseys down in protest of their team owner's racist remarks and thoughts.

Life's Rainbow

A rainbow has colors bright and beautiful.
At its lustrous end there's a pot of gold
leading us to many riches in our lives.

Things of color, like people, are beautiful
also rich in spirit, love, grace, and hope.
They have led us to much greatness in life.

The clouds are white and decorate the sky
creating illusions of what is really there.
Clouds at times come baring heavy storms.

The clouds conceal the rainbow and sunshine
coming into our troubled lives after storms
just as many white people have been telling lies.

Loud Mouth

Known as the mouth of the south
born with a name, means "immortal"
also an item to mold with your hands.

Remembered are the words he spoke
not just rhyme but those of our justice.
Celebrated all his actions; he's immortal.

As he shocks the world with the punch
he dances and his mouth got very loud.
We got to hear him tell how pretty he is.

As he stood on top of the boxing world
with a new name of worthy praise
he'll mold us in ways never done before.

Stood up against a nation for shared beliefs
others were scared said they will take all.
As always, he came out with his hand raise.

Muhammad Ali remembered always!!!

Crumble

A proclamation was signed by him,
yet many tend to ignore the meaning.
They thought of themselves as masters
barriers were built with them mentally.

Years pass, beatings and hangings continue
beautiful people were denounced of self.
Called second-class citizens and walls
were created with their laws to separate.

Yet the blacks would educate and march.
Men named Garvey, X, Washington, King,
Carmichael, Newton, and many more.
Had voices to makes evil walls crumble.

Mockingbird Sings

Through the years the Mockingbird has sung,
From his great perch in a most deafening din.
Many have enjoyed and dance to its tune,
While haters have wished to keep it silent.

Mockingbirds have a rich, gloried and historic past,
Similar to Alexander Crummell, born to former slaves.
The early life of his father shaped his future,
He studied to enrich himself through education.

Crummell work with the Anti-Slavery Society,
Became his song throughout his well-traveled life.
Sang of unity of the black race in many lands,
He influenced W.E.B. Du Bois & Marcus Garvey.

A.T. Welden was also a child of former slaves,
Knew very well of the injustice of black Americans.
His education afforded him a degree in law,
He served in the south to change injustice.

He relentlessly fought for his voting rights,
President of Atlanta's N.A.A.C.P, he sang elegantly.
Proud founder of the Atlanta Negro Voters League,
Believed the Black man had an important voice in politics.

Mockingbird with the well-known and exquisite voice…
Martin Luther King Jr. sang of peace, love, and equality.
He led many marches, and his song soared above all hatred,
Then he was rightfully awarded the Nobel Peace Prize.

These Mockingbirds have been spat on and caged,
Great Mockingbirds of our time have been murdered.
They have at times been called "boy, coon, and nigger…"

We shall live the dream and call one, "Mr. President!"

CONGRATULATIONS BARACK OBAMA!

Mother's Milk

A mother will feed her infant milk
her young a glass with their meal
tell them it makes their bones strong.

Growing kids would learn much on
Mother's teaching of faith and truth
through the word, love, and discipline.

Upon learning the Almighty's word
Mother sends her children to be teachers.
Stumble and fall they come back to mother.

She's there, as always, with Mother's Milk
to strengthen the bones and teach the basics.
Build a strong foundation for God's children.

Hebrews 5:12

Milkmaid

My mother is the milkmaid of the family
bringing the milk, making our bones strong.
Her love and care has been the milk for us;
a great vitamin D for our bodies and minds.

She is full of good faith and lively spirits
knowing a joyful heart is good medicine.
Healing through her hands and the Lord
always the milk pours over and into the body.

Bringing her family to the house of the Lord
letting the word be the milk for the bones.
Her love and care with the Lord's word keeps
spirits up knowing broken spirits dry bones.

Proverbs 17:22

No Blacks Allowed

There's a big issue that will never die,
one of ownership and great superiority.
Sits there in his seat overlooking his ship;
he sees his slave ship with a different look.

Such great men of color will run and sweat
to play a game of massive fun for others.
Making this evil man millions of dollars
as he feels it is their duty to do so for him.

Will proclaim it is not his way of thinking
Yet, the way this world thinks it should be.
So he tells his lady of great beauty and fun
it's ok to like and sleep with them in private.

Yet, in his mind of power and dominance…
The way him and his club of men of hatred
see it, this is the N.B.A.
No Blacks Allowed!!!

Path before Me

The path before me was laid by my mother
when she placed a great leader in front of us.
My sister has trained our minds to make us smarter,
fed our bodies to grow stronger in times of need.

We had fallen; you extended your right hand to us
My older sibling faces our strongest adversary
while training us to fight battles through God.
She gave us a righteous and holy shield of victory.

My sister broadened the path for us to walk upon.
She was our salvation protecting us from harm.
We would never turn to evil if we fell, we only
became stronger while on the path to righteousness.

Psalm 18:35-36

Don't You Worry

I stand here with heartfelt tears.
Yet your words to me & others,
"Don't you worry about me."

It's then I would come to realize
the sweet songbird is going home.
The harps are being tuned up and
there will be many songs of jubilation.

Yes we now cry,
many are without dry eyes.
Stay strong and not say goodbye,
because in our hearts you remain.

We will not worry…
The sweet songbird is going home,
to share that voice with angels above.
Home is where you belong.

Queen's Crown

Your ancestors have been removed
from their mother land long ago.
The crown removed from their heads.
Yet, royalty remains in the bloodline.

You are Queen Mother, Governess of many.
Mother of character, education, and beauty
They've taken a crown of glimmer and jewels,
yet, your value always shines through evil.

The crown on your head now is your hair,
you wear it with pride in honor of self.
Never in vain, yet to show the queen you are.
I bow in honor; you have taught us much.

So wear your crown as you wish and desire,
It will never diminish the person that you are
We all know the great leader you are for us,
so stand proud with your head above many.

Days of Yesterday
(Hate Version)

Those days of yesterday
To have them back again
What we call the Golden Age

No one would step out of line
They were much too scared Yes!
When a boy knew his place

Always asking for things
Wasn't enough we freed them from slavery
Even gave up 40 acres and a mule

We have been a little tough
Do they deserve some things?
Only what we allow them

Put them in school
Give some people education
Plumb lose their mind
Now want to be called Sir or Madam
Show some kind of respect
Remember when a nigger was a nigger

Let's get back to yesterday
Build on our tomorrow
Power to the right people.

Days of Yesterday

Days of yesterday
Spiritual and uplifting
Togetherness created change

Feeling shackled with freedom
Riding in the back of the bus
Drinking from a different fountain

Color of someone's skin
Could scare so many
Lower level education, different restaurant

Marching hand in hand, singing songs
Will not ride that bus
Fighting for respect

Change starting to come
While we withstood fire hoses and dogs
Beating with batons and jail

We must remember
The fight of those before us
Working together makes things better

Thanks to some people's dream
We live a better life
In each of them I honor
Let's get back to yesterday
To steady build our tomorrow
Power to all people.

Questions

As they murder the fatherless;
we come with many questions.
Yet, none are to you dear Lord.

Appointed who we thought wise
to make the decisions of justice.
It is they who have a blind eye.

March and make cries for truth;
while department heads turn deaf.
Do they lack your knowledge Lord?
Evildoers are arrogant and boast;
we will continue to stand in faith.
God sees and knows all doings.

The wicked will soon be punished
true judgment is always served.
Evil cannot hide behind their power.

Psalm 94 1-13

Grandma's Secret

Psst! Grandma had called me over;
said let me tell you a nice little secret.
The secret was about my superb mom.

I already held her in the highest honors
she had the tightest afro and dashiki
her bellbottoms rang; my mother dress cool.

What my grandma told me was that my
mother was visited by a sun angel before.
I was in awe I couldn't believe my ears.

Grandma pulled me to the window to
show me mother and said if you look
at her in a certain light she has a glow.

Mother had powers, made pains go away
when we were sick she made us better.
Put great food on an empty dinner table.

She never did change water into wine
the warmth she provided was sunshine.
All she did for everyone seem like miracles.

Grandma Rain

My grandmother was rain to the family;
she was the nourishment of love for us.
Drip, drip, drip, just a little for the babies
then she would open up as we all grew.

Raining down righteousness on all around
being honorable to God and family always.
Showering love having a home of salvation
protecting for evils of the hatred world around.

As she was the rain that cause things to grow;
my grandmother was warmth for a scared soul.
She gave me a light in darkness to find a way
showed us the true light is through God's word.

Bless her monsoon over us.
Isaiah 45:8

Racist Bullet

The racist bullet been around for a long time
Taking out men of many different skin tones
Yet, it is always when it supports men of dark.

Racist bullet put into Abraham Lincoln's head
Because he changed the lives of 3 million people,
In the single stroke on a piece of beautiful paper

A racist bullet smashed in Martin Luther King Jr.'s jaw
Yet, nothing will ever silence the words of this man
They ring forever in our ears and we will march on.

Today the racist bullets are in those behind the badge
We see the revolution is being televised and on Facebook
Let's continue to have a voice and make them accountable.

Riches

We were not a family of riches
yet, we were spoiled with love.
The needs were surely provided.

Mother would not spare the rod
discipline was applied when needed;
she pampered with toys and clothes.

Abundant family love from many hearts,
feeding food and affection to the kids.
They knowing not of the troubled times.

Kids are in church on Sunday morning.
Teaching kids love of family and self.
Love of God, family, and self is rich in itself.

Falling Walls

As if their own trumpet had sounded
cue to sing their song of hateful glee.

Would boast; own chest they pounded
They'd rather see you hung from a tree.

Much evil carried down for many years
covenant of war between man, not God.

Drank wine then made chats and cheers
truth came; gave themselves much applause.

They sounded their horns for many to hear
the walls of hate were soon to start falling.

Walls of false brotherhood would disappear
hate will always fall; it is the Almighty calling.

Satisfy

Satisfaction is not what you seek
it is something you already have.
Look within and around, then smile.

Many complain of work they do now
yet, you have a job and be thankful.
Pray talents awarded by God to rise.

You cry for new clothing and shelter
there are textiles on your back and feet
roof over your head others have none.

You have come to the Lord in true faith.
He has provided for you abundantly
realize God satisfies all who come in.

Continue to give in tithes to the house
pray to the Lord Almighty in true faith.
Blessings rain down satisfaction guaranteed.
Psalm 22:26

Stained Glass

There it stood on 16th street,
oldest black church in the city.
In a municipality much divided
on its long history of unjust hate.

Terrorism alive in the deep south
from Americans with nasty venom.
Preying on others because of skin,
lives beaten and always taken away.

There's this beautiful place of God
standing with its lovely stained glass;
where God's youngest children have
now come to sing, praise, and worship.

The thunder rolled and shook the city;
everyone knowing something's not right.
To learn 16th Street church has been bombed
there's glass and cement embedded in heads.

A place of love, worship, and embrace
bombed because of evil hostility of a race.
Glass once decorated with beautiful colors
now stained with the blood of God's children.

Night Walk

It's a clear humid spring night
as he walks home from his job.
Reflecting on events of the day
also those of his ancestors past.

A beautiful night's sky lit up bright
full moon and stars light his way.
He looks to the distance, walking
along thinks of the progress made.

A car passes screaming obscenities
throwing bottles, his night is shaken.
Evil coming in the darkness of night
drunkenness bringing out buried hate.

Psalm 82:5

Daily Wealth

We were a household of low income
mother always spoke of truth and grace.
Learning the Lord's word every Sunday.

Mother said as we build moral character
our name comes into strong standing.
We would have daily favor in our lives.

Daily we close the day on bended knee Lord
bless us with our needs answered
having a wealth of guardianship from above.

Church on Sunday was a great time of praise
afterwards we are at family house together
at a table sharing food, wealth and much love.

Realize daily wealth of the Lord
comes at no trouble through faith.

Proverbs 10:22, 19:22

Stirred

Our hearts have often been stirred
by beautiful words of the gifted.
Whether they are spoken or written.
Queen Angelou moved us to think.

Many speak yet say nothing.
When the queen spoke or wrote
we were tuned in to be enlightened.
Using God-given gifts for a purpose.

Hand and mind were very skillful,
the tongue of a genius just as much.
Spoke of many things in this world;
of evil and injustice always of truth.

Gracious words always delivered;
because it was the gifts of an angel.
Queen Angelou is on her way home
To be with the Almighty....

To recite a poem. Psalm 45: 1-4

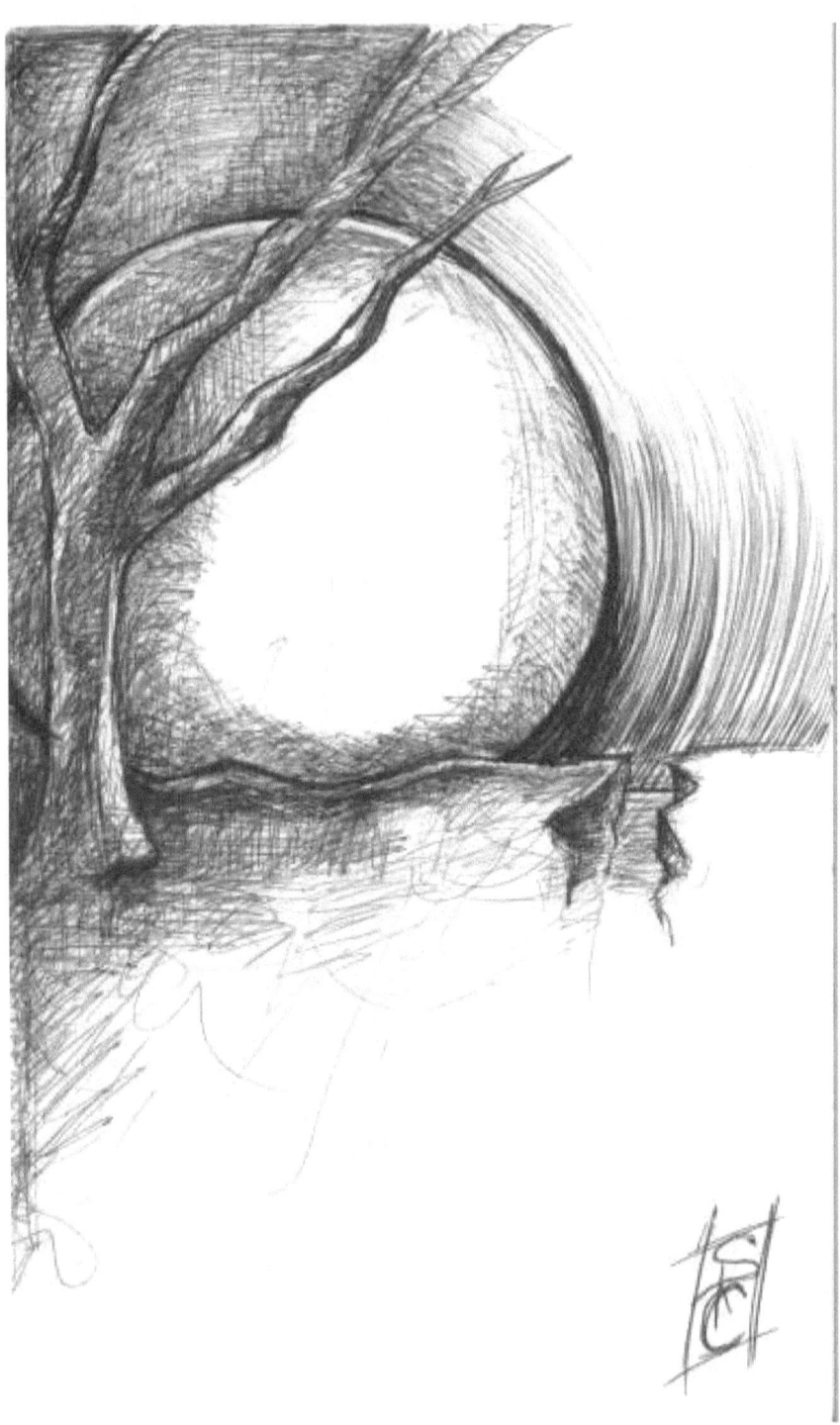

Spanish Moss

Spanish moss on Southern Live Oak
is not a growth established on the tree.
Yet, it is the tears the tree now cries
from lives it has helped take in the past.

The moss hangs long and steadfast
as the innocent lives of many blacks.
So the Oak now cries consistently
remembering lives from its branch.

Live Oak always asks itself, "Why?"
Why so strong; why so many lives?
Just a tree minding my own business
up came the rope with a hanging body.

Meant to carve a couples' name into
to have a colorful picnic of great love.
Even give a protester an endearing hug.
Never to take a life out of a man's hate.

Therefore, now hang tears of Spanish moss.

Stained

Living with a 245-year old blemish
on the history of my ancestors.
Their blood stains the ground
of the mother land removed from.

Chained in the bowels of a ship
as tears and sweat tarnish the wood.
Someone else's prized commodities
to be sold to many evil lazy bigots.

Some of the worst stains of all
were on the wipes used to beat;
on the cotton and tobacco leaves
of the blood of kings and queens.

Sheets are stained from raping's
taken upon innocent women and girls.
The evils of slavery are horrible
for the blood shed I cry many tears.

Unknown Sharecroppers

Taken from a land they called home
put on a ship chained head to toe;
on an auction block sometimes naked
to be sold to a man call himself master.
Names of homeland matter no more
given new name of man with whip.
Working hard in a field under hot sun
produce a crop of vast worth and need.
Agriculture growth of a young nation
its sharecroppers grew with it also.
They worked harder producing more
under the sun for the foreign demand.
Much money was made from crops grown
none never for the unknown sharecropper.
The only thing they were sharing was blood
on the beds from the rapes and fields for labor.

Unto Others

Lord understand what I'm about to do.
You said do onto others as you
would have them do onto you.
So my actions only are shared force.

White man for long has abused his powers
has beaten and broken the black man bones.
Called him nigger, a word of no meaning;
denied equal education and housing to many.

My question is why he would treat others like this
because if he is doing to others as they would
in turn do onto him, would he like this treatment?
I don't mean to be evil Lord, it's just payback.

Tarnish

As we now listen to the evil
spoken words of the rich.
We cry out for swift justice;
To fall upon one this evil man.

His name once shined like silver.
It is tarnish from his tongue.
Pockets of hateful have fattened;
Off the vile actions of this man

So his tarnished name now burns.
Everyone now sees him for the
person many claimed him to be.
Their cries are heard by all now.

James 5:1-6

Authors Comments:

I am speaking of Donald Sterling the former owner of the L.A. Clippers; who for years many have claimed to be racist. He has been sued for denying housing to Blacks & Latinos; a case settled out of court. He also sued by former player Elgin Baylor for age discrimination. His downfall finally came when he was caught on tape saying he did not want Blacks attending Clippers' games. That is when he did not shine anymore. He was tarnish and force out of the league.

Stolen Dreams

First we ask for development of our minds
better to mix, inspire, and grow together.
Whites lived their dream with no blacks.

Decision made for a better education
angered many people they want no part.
Blacks had handed down books.

Angry and poor sitting next to a black
yet, if they worked hard it would all end.
They would soon live the American dream.

Year later whites are still poor and angry
in jobs where the boss' skin is a darker hue.
They feel their American dream's been stolen.

Grandma's Tablecloth

In mother's kitchen the other day
passed by her nice fancy table with
its runner and charger plates...Wow!
Nice enough to be in some magazine.

What was missing was a tablecloth;
Grandma's table was covered for sure.
Had its centerpiece, shakers, and napkins.
The most precious was the checkered cloth.

Had coffee stains from the morning brew;
A few cigarette burns were to be found.
It held warm pots and casserole dishes
also held cold glasses of Kool-Aid or water.

Most of all it held loving family memories;
those words of grace and thanks to God.
On a quiet day alone drinking coffee
you'll close your eyes and hear laugher.

When Work Is Fun

When you are a kid 100° outside
is not something you feel on you.
It's a joy to help out on the farm,
you're now part of the family meals.

Sister in the kitchen with grandma
apron on, making dough for biscuits.
Grandma's strong hands mend on and
soft hands when she helps you bathe.

You and brother with grandpa outside
in your overalls ready to ring chicken necks.
Strong wrist as he twists that chicken around
gentle as he helps you with your Sunday tie.

Hot summer day as you snap green beans
then husk the fresh silky yellow corn.
Grandkids on front porch hand churn ice cream
Heat matters, unfinished work settles all that.
When the work is done for family and love,
It is nothing but welcomed and fun.
Yet, when it is being done to pay bills
makes it bitter and very unrewarding.

Devil's Badge

Made a promise to protect and serve
yet, it was his lie to get the shiny badge.
The devil served no one but himself
would make no promise to God above.

So he patrolled looking for his prey,
rolled four deep to the side you went.
People of color he had an attraction for
his baton, kept taken to them very often.

Devil fell in love with his found power
it came often it became very excessive.
He began to take many lives quickly,
paid no price for it in the land of man.

Clever disguise an angel of light to protect
many saw through its video to prove.
Justice would not do anything as the
devil did genocide of a nation of people.

2 Corinthians 11:3

Section 2

THROUGH THE FIRE (TRIBUTE TO MY SON MICHAEL GRENZER)

Awaken

My son awakens from a nightmare
it becomes reality with me there.
I'm not supposed to be here now
have not been much before.

Awaken wrapped like a mummy
skin burned and withered away.
My son worries how to carry on
I assure him in time he'll be healed.

My presence has been seasonal
my love is like the word of the Lord
enduring it will last forever.
I'll be here until he walks out.

1Peter 1-24-25

Complete

We should always be honored with joy when
God puts his servant through trials.
It's only for us to grow and make complete.

God knew of the great tragedy to my son
before it accorded because He sees all.
He knows it's a trial for father and son.

I had true faith just did not know when.
Doctors did work to make his skin complete
I had patience; prayed for healing in God's time.

Having faith and patience I became blessed
seeing my son wake with the crown of life.
Knowing family, love of God has pulled through.

Faith, patience, and hard work will make us complete
James 1:2-4, 12

Many Hands

We are seeing many hands come together
in this great time of sorrow in our hearts.
Showing love and support for your servant.

Hands come together in prayer to you Lord
as your blessing will come down upon us.
We thank you now for the miracles coming.

Kept lungs smoke free and swelling down
Now take flesh and cover with new skin
Then breathe your new life into it my Lord.

Healing takes time Lord give us your strength
To carry through this long process, we trust in
you as these many hands come together

Ezekiel 37-6

Neighborhood

It appeared to be a beautiful day for me,
the sun was shining in my neighborhood.
Working among friends, we're all smiling.

Then came a call that great disaster struck,
clouds of tears over took my neighborhood.
my son was far away I needed to be by his side.

Never forsaken by my brothers and sisters
they worked hard through this awful disaster.
To offer me a new living zip code with my son.

The new neighborhood was full of pain
yet, across the way I saw determination
making it a beautiful day in the neighborhood.

Proverbs 27:10

Righteous

There was a righteous man stricken
then confined to bed by great extent.
Much pain through body and heart.

Yet when he awakens from slumber
he speaks truth with his kind soul.
Righteous this man of mass virtue.

True instruction given to make whole
once again by teacher and sick man.
When walked, it was in great peace.

Believing in himself and working hard,
what you do for yourself is what matters.
A man walking with great integrity.

Malachi 2:6
Psalm 15:2

Superb

My son is a very superb black man
in him is the blood of his forefathers.
Who withstood 245-years old of slavery.
Made it through the Jim Crow years.

Our superb forefathers who held sanity
their dignity through all the beatings.
A strong belief that God would pull them
through the selling and stealing from home.

When slavery ended and hanging began
they would march and fight to be equal.
Sing songs saying we're just as good if
not better; black is beautiful, I'm proud.

So when my son is faced with adversity
he would get that superb blood flowing.
Work hard! Not afraid to sweat a little.
Then he is making mom and dad proud.

Together

We were brought back together
through a terrible misfortune in life
Frightened by the event of great dread.

Together is loving father and son;
body weakened by fires of misfortune.
Strengthened by Michael's determination.

God knows the when; He knows all;
Michael always believing in himself
Together in faith Father and Son walk

Two men walking and healing together
through the strength of the energetic son.
Communion with God's love and healing.

Amos 3:3

Section 3

SAD & PAINFUL

Cry for You

You said you were touched in places,
that no adult should ever touch a kid.
Because of these actions,
I cry for you now!

I'm sorry that you were scared,
no child should live with hatred and fear!
Do not be angry at yourself, you did nothing wrong.
Fear not the person who claims love for you.

No need to worry,
your soul is pure.
They face eternal damnation!
For that I cheer for you!

I can't take back what has happened,
sorry I can't take away the pain.
You do not have to cry anymore.
I will cry for you.

Since I could not help,
I WILL CRY FOR YOU!

Demons

Evil living among us,
walking & smiling trying to befriend.
Wearing mask, fooling everyone.

If this is love, "why?"
Do I hurt so much,
Feel so dirty?

I want to scream,
"Please stop doing this
I do not like it!"

I want to tell someone, "but who?"
Will they hurt me also?
They claim to love me too…

There are no monsters in the closet,
None hiding under the bed.
They sit at the Thanksgiving table.

Hugging me longer than most.
Smiling at me with evil eyes,
Touching me in places I do not like.

Yes, this will be stopped!
Time to make a stand...
Their Demons will be exorcised!

Not because of my love for them,
Because I love myself.
I am special. I am somebody!

Author's Comments:

This is for those who have endured pain and evil that most of us never thought could exist. I Love You All!! For your pain, I still "Cry For You" For those new to my work, this is a follow up to "Cry For You"

Demon's Cry

Sun setting in the distance along the coast,
beautiful rainbow hews of violet red and blue.
Calmness of the moment does not fill you,
you are consumed with sadness and grief.

Sun setting brings the darkness of the night.
The night is for the demons that haunt you,
demons that preyed on your sweet innocence.
You lie there and cry hoping for the best.

The tears do not flow down your face,
it is your heart that cries out for you.
Lay there eyes closed and shaking with fear,
your pity no one hears and comes to comfort.

This evil robbed you of a happy childhood,
brought you down into the depths of hell.
Seen and feared things no human should encounter,
all of this from the early stages of life.

I look into your beautiful eyes!
I see the pain inside of your heart,
you try to hide it and bury it deep.
It's my weight to bear now.

I open my heart to fill you with love,
exorcize these demons from your life.
I embrace you in God's comfort and love.
You need not to cry anymore.

I shall cry for you.

Crime Scene

Been known as the entertainment king. Look
ing out for no one's gain but yourself.
Uncontrolled advance when told do not cross.
Silent no more real heroes have now spoken.
Her body was a crime scene from your actions.

Women who once hid tremendous pain and truth.
I now cry their tears they should be free now.
Nobody!... is your name now as you head to hell.
Everybody knows the truth behind your evil smile.

Section 4

MARY'S GOODBYE

Holding On

Boy in life my mother had a strong hold.
Listen to my words she said they are wise.
Understand I will help do as you're told.
She said take her right hand for guidance.
Her lessons hurt at times when you disobeyed.
Yet when you followed the reward great as gold.

We remember holding on to life in that bed.
With a strong grip in her weak hand not going.
Fighting death like Rocky kept getting back up.
I remember that grip as a 35 yr. old on my shirt.
She asks before 'You Know who I am?'
When I oppose her, she was never defected.
Now we love this winner yet knows what's ahead.
Everyone celebrates the life of Mary Bates.

We're holding on to the love she carried.
Holding on to the great memories.

Mary Satisfies

Been outside looking Mary took you in.
Living in her home as if it was yours.
Ultimate fest: all she asked was no sin.
She would clothe your back with a smile.
Her home: is your home Mary was to satisfy

We were always full of food, water, and love.
In style with a smile, you sure to step.
None greater the Lord said satisfy My children.
Everyone loves what you did; you'll a white dove.

Home now at peace in the promise kingdom.
You can recruit for God now till you are eighty.
Sure to ask last time you sin & are you on your path.

Thanks Mary, we love you dearly!

Matthew 25:34-40

Fighting In Faith

Been leader all our lives I know you fight in faith.
Lord it's in your hands the ones of miracles now.
Understand your wishes are to be done this time.
Strengthen the damage make it all new again Lord.
Healing like You always done make us saw...Wow!

We've seen the damage just say 'Breathe Mary'
In faith she lies in fighting, ready to be with family.
The front doors she came for healing so let it be.
Everyone ready for the welcome home praise Jesus party

Mother's Voice

Business was my mother's sweet voice;
Loving was every word that she spoke.
Ultimate determination it meant all.
She got your attention right away,
Her job was to take over your ear.

We were captivated by her angelic voice.
I'm a book reader because of her trips.
No place like the world of mother's voice.
Everyone loves the stern yet loving sound.
Forever endured will be miss always.

Strong As Oak

Blood in your veins is like the water of life.
Lamb of God bless Mary Bates with a miracle.
Ultimate control is in your healing hands.
Strong as oak is she we love her dearly!
Here is the Tree of Life to represent a queen.

We bow in prayer each leaf has healing power.
In her will walk the vibrant woman we know.
Now breath into her lungs Lord retore them now.
Everyone says glory hallelujah; we honor you & her.

Seeking Answers

Been seeking answers all my course.
Looked to my mother a lady of wisdom.
Ultimate knowledge a powerful source!
She led everyone on the path of righteous.
Her home was your home, a true provider.

We come seeking answers for life troubles.
In Mary's heart of love was your answers.
None greater than a lady of God on your side.
Everyone full of food and knowledge.
Thanks Mary!

About the Author

Kevin Bates was born in Beaumont, Texas and currently resides in Houston, TX. A devoted reader and writer; each day is spent wandering in the world of words. As a kid his mother brought him into the world of words. "She would read with her sweet angelic voice taking me so far away doing things I never done before. Living the adventures of the people she read about. Soon afterward when I asked her to read another she would tell me to pick a book off the shelf & to read it myself."

Through reading, Kevin learned early that words are powerful when shared correctly through speech or in print. His mission is to share his message with you, "so we all can come to a common understanding throughout the world and to be your brother under God."

OTHER BOOKS BY KEVIN BATES

Sweet Emotions
ABC's of Love

CONNECT WITH KEVIN HERE:

Website: http://www.kevinwbates.com/
Facebook: Kevin.Bates.940
Twitter: Kevin_W_Bates
Blog: https://kevsworld.org
Youtube: Kevin Bates

www.ingramcontent.com/pod-product-compliance
Lightning Source LLC
Chambersburg PA
CBHW030313130626
46549CB00002B/830